I AM DETERMINED TO PROVE TO MYSELF WHAT I'M TRULY CAPABLE OF.

Stronger THAN YOUR excuses

PERFECT BODY LOADING... please wait

TRAVEL BRINGS ME A LEVEL OF PEACE THAT IS INCOMPARABLE

ADVENTURES

WORKOUT

I HONOR MY BODY BY STAYING ACTIVE AND FIT

Hello 2024

VISION BOARD
Clip Art Book
FOR GIRLS

LET THE Adventure BEGIN

DREAM, DISCOVER, TRAVEL

NO GOAL was met WITHOUT a little SWEAT

MY HOME WARM

welcome HOME

Health is Wealth

FOOD DIET

choose Healthy

Healthy food Healthy life

Health and Beauty

Health Day

I HAVE A SANCTUARY IN MY HOME, JUST FOR ME

HOME

LIVE IN A RELAXING, INSPIRING ENVIRONMENT

MY BODY IS SACRED AND I WILL TAKE CARE OF IT

HEALTHY EATING

I EAT FOOD TO NOURISH AND CELEBRATE MY BODY

Healthy Life

TRAVEL BRINGS ME A LEVEL OF PEACE THAT IS INCOMPARABLE

ADVENTURES

MY JOURNEY TO NEW DESTINATIONS IS ALWAYS PEACEFUL AND REWARDING

I AM A STRONG INDIVIDUAL WHO ATTRACTS SUCCESS AND HAPPINESS

HOBBIES

I CHOOSE TO THINK POSITIVELY AND CREATE A WONDERFUL AND SUCCESSFUL LIFE FOR MYSELF

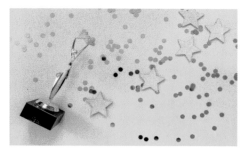

12 NEW Chapters 365 CHANCES

I am confident

YOUR YEAR Is Waiting GO GET IT

YOUR NEXT Chapter Is GOING TO BE amazing

LET'S TOAST TO YESTERDAY'S Achievements And TOMORROW'S bright future

LEARN FROM Yesterday Live FOR TODAY HOPE For Tomorrow

MY GREATEST GLORY IS IN RISING UP EVERY TIME I FAIL

Achievements

I WORK HARD AT WHAT IS IMPORTANT TO ME AND I ACCOMPLISH AMAZING THINGS!

Knowledge Has A Beginning BUT NO END

TODAY I DO WHAT OTHERS DON'T, So Tomorrow I Can Do What Others Can't!

EXPAND YOURSELF

I AM FIRMLY On The Path Of Achievement

Hooray!

I'M DONE

I'm just out here *trusting* **GOD**

I KNOW THAT I
EXIST FOR A
DIVINE
PURPOSE

SPIRITUALITY

I KNOW THAT
GOD HAS GIVEN
ME THE POWER
TO HELP
MYSELF

LOVE LIKE JESUS

GOD IS GOOD
all the time

Just Jesus

PRAY on it
PRAY over it
PRAY through it

LOVE GOD
love people

love like
JESUS

with
GOD
all things are possible

FAITH
over
FEAR

GOD
IS GOOD
all the time

you are enough

JESUS
Best gift ever

FAITH CAN MOVE
MOUNTAINS

I HATE
NOTHING
ABOUT U

I Love
you

love

I AM ATTRACTING
THE PERFECT
PERSON FOR ME

RELATIONSHIP

I DESERVE TO BE
HAPPY IN MY
RELATIONSHIP

BRANDING

→ IDENTITY
→ LOGO
→ DESIGN
→ STRATEGY
→ MARKETING

I AM WORTHY OF RECEIVING ABUNDANT REWARDS FOR MY HARD WORK

BUSINESS

I AM OPEN TO RECEIVING UNEXPECTED WINDFALLS AND FINANCIAL BLESSINGS

SAY «NO» TO THINGS YOU HATE

ready FOR BIGGER and BETTER things

Put YOUR ideas OUT INTO THE WORLD

Put your LIPSTICK on and HUSTLE

Work HARD SHOW THEM!

THIS IS THE SIGN YOU'VE BEEN WAITING FOR

THE SECRET to getting ahead is GETTING STARTED

Surround YOURSELF with POSITIVE PEOPLE

MY HOME IS RADIANT WITH WARM, INVITING ENERGY

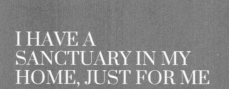

I HAVE A SANCTUARY IN MY HOME, JUST FOR ME

HOME

LIVE IN A RELAXING, INSPIRING ENVIRONMENT

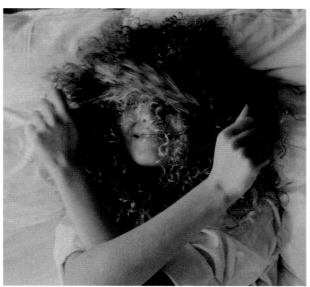

FRIENDS
MAKE THE WORLD A
beautiful
PLACE

Yes, i'm that FRIEND

True friendship *is seen through* THE HEART *not through* THE EYES

To have a friend and be a friend is what makes life worthwhile

I WILL MAKE MY FRIENDSHIPS BEAUTIFUL AND FULFILLING

FRIENDS

I CAN RELY ON MY FRIENDS FOR SUPPORT, EMOTIONAL OR OTHERWISE

IT'S NOT WHAT WE HAVE IN LIFE, BUT WHO WE HAVE *that matters*

MY FRIENDS ARE MY *therapy*

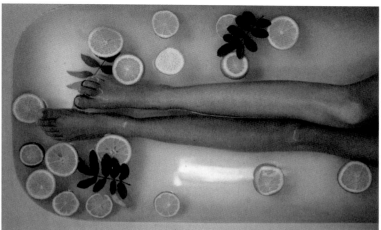

BE KIND

THERE IS A BEAUTIFUL LOVING LIGHT INSIDE OF ME

SELFCARE

I TAKE GREAT CARE OF MY BODY

I CAN HANDLE MASSIVE
SUCCESS WITH EASE

FINANCE

MY CAPACITY TO HOLD
AND GROW MONEY
EXPANDS EVERY DAY

I AM DETERMINED TO PROVE TO MYSELF WHAT I'M TRULY CAPABLE OF.

Stronger
★ **THAN** ★
YOUR
excuses

PERFECT BODY
LOADING...
please wait

I DESERVE TO INVEST IN MY HEALTH AND FITNESS JOURNEY

WORKOUT

I HONOR MY BODY BY STAYING ACTIVE AND FIT

THE BODY
Achieves
WHAT
The mind
BELIEVES

NO GOAL
was met
WITHOUT
a little
SWEAT

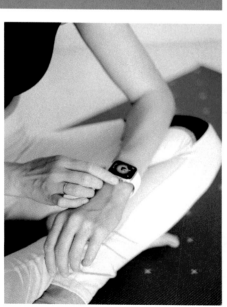

HEALTHY EATING
IS A WAY OF LIFE

SO IT'S IMPORTANT TO ESTABLISH ROUTINES

THAT ARE SIMPLE

REALISTICALLY AND ULTIMATELY LIVABLE

HEALTHY FOOD

choose Healthy

Health and Beauty

Health Day

Healthy food Healthy life

Health IS Wealth

FOOD DIET VEGETABLES NUTRITION DIETARY LOW

MY BODY IS SACRED AND I WILL TAKE CARE OF IT

HEALTHY EATING

I EAT FOOD TO NOURISH AND CELEBRATE MY BODY

Healthy Life

dreams Don't Work UNLESS You Do

Use Your mistakes To Build STAIRS Not Walls

Work HARD Pray HARDER

WHO YOU ARE Tomorrow Begins With WHAT YOU DO today

Work For A Cause Not For Applause

I NEVER Dreamed ABOUT SUCCESS I Worked FOR IT

AM DETERMINED TO BE SUCCESSFUL AT WORK

WORK

I AM THE AUTHOR OF MY OWN SUCCESS STORY

NEVER STOP WORKING

idea

CREATIVE STARTUP

Say Yes To new adventures

BONUS IMAGES & ELEMENTS

Growth is growth, no matter how small.

Turn challenges into changes and stress into **success.**

Be your own happy ever after.

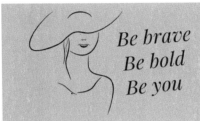

Be brave
Be bold
Be you

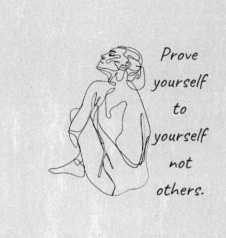

Prove yourself to yourself not others.

STOP STOPING YOURSELF.

Create a life you can't wait to wake up to.

Remember this dear, if you plays small, you stay small.

You're more than what you think.

ARE YOU MOTIVATED ENOUGH?

If opportunity doesn't knock, build a door.

Be stronger than your excuses.

Look at everything you have over come, Don't give up now.

MY VOICE, MY OPINION, AND MY TRUTH MATTER AND SHOULD BE HEARD

I ACCEPT MYSELF AND MY FLAWS, THEY ARE WHAT MAKES ME WHO I AM

I WILL ONLY COMPARE MYSELF WITH THE BEST VERSION OF MYSELF

I BELIEVE IN ME AND
IN WHAT I AM
CAPABLE OF DOING

I COMBINE FEMININITY
AND INTELLIGENCE
BEAUTIFULLY

I COMMIT TO LIVING
A JOYFUL AND
HAPPY LIFE

ultimate
BOSS
babe

GIRL·BOSS
girl boss
GIRL·BOSS
girl boss

I AM STRONG
BECAUSE
A STRONG
woman
Raised Me

where there is no
STRUGGLE
there is no
Strength

You
DON'T KNOW
How
STRONG
YOU ARE
UNTIL BEING
STRONG
is the only
CHOICE YOU HAVE

She has
FIRE
in her
SOUL &
GRACE

SPOIL ME
with
LOYALTY I CAN
FINANCE
MYSELF

she
is far more
PRECIOUS
then rubies

strong
women
RAISE
strong
Girls

UNDERESTIMATE
ME
THAT WILL BE
FUN

YOU WERE GIVEN
THIS LIFE
because
YOU ARE
STRONG
ENOUGH TO
LIVE IT

YOU
Totally
GOT THIS
GIRL

I CAN ACCOMPLISH
ANYTHING I SET MY
MIND TO

EVERYWHERE I GO, I
ATTRACT JOY AND
HAPPINESS

THE UNIVERSE'S
HEALING POWER
FLOWS THROUGH
ALL THE CELLS OF
MY BODY

GIRL
you have
NO IDEA
how
Strong you are

Don't be
Discouraged

You Were
GIVEN
this life

turn all this
Pain
INTO
Power

NOT FRAGILE
like a
FLOWER
fragile
like a
BOMB

yes
YOU
can

brave
AND
strong

the hustle IS REAL

»»»STOP Trying

≈STOP making EXCUSES≈

MAKE»»» THINGS ≈HAPPEN≈

Make YOURSELF Proud

LIFE IS SHORT

LIFE IS BEAUTIFUL

BE BRAVE

Kindness IS ALWAYS FREE

≈DREAM WITHOUT FEAR≈

never lose hope

AFTER EVERY ★STORM★ THERE IS A RAINBOW

I AM BRAVE, I AM LOVED, I AM GOOD ENOUGH

I AM BEAUTIFUL AND PERFECT THE WAY I AM, NO ONE CAN TELL ME OTHERWISE

MY EXQUISITE FEMALE BODY RADIATES LOVING KINDNESS TO THE WORLD

BE STILL AND know THAT I AM GOD

BE MINDFUL BE Grateful BE KIND BE POSITIVE

BREATHE, DARLING This is Just a Chapter NOT THE WHOLE Story

Doubt KILLS MORE DREAMS THAN FAILURE EVER WILL

DO WHAT MAKES YOUR Soul SHINE

CHAOS Coordinator

Faith hope Love

Even the DARKEST NIGHT ENDS AND THE SUN RISES AGAIN

GOD IS IN CONTROL

GRATEFUL MIND GRATEFUL Vibes GREAT LIFE

SO, Apparently I HAVE an ATTITUDE

START THIS DAY thinking ABOUT ALL THAT YOU ARE INSTEAD OF ALL THAT YOU ARE not

START THIS DAY WITH A GRATEFUL heart

THANKFULNESS IS THE Quickest PATH TO Joy

TRUST THE timing OF YOUR LIFE

WHEN YOU focus ON THE GOOD THE GOOD INCREASES

WITH GOD ALL THINGS ARE POSSIBLE

YOU WILL Never READY BE JUST START

I CAN DO ALL Things through CHRIST WHO STRENGTHENS ME

YOU WILL Never READY BE JUST START

YOU ARE Enough

IT'S A marathon NOT A SPRINT YOU'RE ON THE RIGHT TRACK

I AM RESPONSIBLE FOR MY HAPPINESS

I AM GRATEFUL FOR THIS LIFE I HAVE BEEN GIVEN

I CAN REACH ALL OF MY GOALS IF I SET MY MIND TO IT

IT DOESN'T GET EASIER YOU JUST GET STRONGER

IT IS WELL WITH MY Soul

SIMPLY Blessed

KEEP Going KEEP Growing

ONE FOOT forward ONE DAY AT A TIME

MAKE TODAY Amazing

SHE BELIEVED SHE COULD SO SHE did

Thankful GRATEFUL Blessed

Thank you!

We are thrilled to extend our heartfelt gratitude for your recent purchase of our **Vision Board Clip Art Book for Girls**. Your support means the world to us, and we can't wait for you to explore the creative possibilities that await within its pages.

We believe that creating a vision board is an incredible journey towards manifesting your dreams and goals. With this clip art book, we aimed to provide you with a toolkit to make that journey even more exciting and visually engaging. We trust that the vibrant illustrations and versatile elements will empower your vision board to truly reflect your aspirations.

As you dive into your creative projects, we kindly request your feedback. Your thoughts are invaluable to us and to others who are considering enhancing their creative process with our book. If you have a moment to spare, we would greatly appreciate it if you could share your experience and insights in a few words on Amazon. Your honest review will help fellow dreamers make informed decisions and discover the magic of our **Vision Board Clip Art Book for Girls**.

Wishing you endless inspiration and success as you craft your vision board masterpiece in 2024!

Warm regards,
Jasmine Eason

Made in the USA
Las Vegas, NV
04 January 2024

83842468R00026